D1236195

YOU

Make my Day

STEPHEN MARSHALL

You Make My Day
31 Ways To Your Best Days
Copyright information

Unless otherwise noted, Scripture quotations are taken from the King James Version of the Bible.

Scripture quotations noted TLB are from The Living Bible, Copyright ©1971. Used by permission of Tyndale House Publishers, Inc. Wheaton, Illinois 60189. All rights reserved.

Scripture quotations noted NLT are from the New Living Translation, Copyright ©1996. Used by permission of Tyndale House Publishers, Inc Wheaton, Illinois 60189. All rights reserved.

Scripture quotations marked AMPLIFIED are taken from The Amplified Bible. Copyright © 1987 by The Zondervan Corporation and the Lockman Foundation, Grand Rapids, Michigan. Used by permission.

Copyright ©2005 by Stephen Marshall Allison

ISBN 0-938020-82-X

First printing 2005

Editor: Cristel Phelps
Illustrations by Ron Wheeler
Cover & book design by Lindsay Allison

Published by Decapolis Publishing
Printed in the United States of America

written by
Stephen
MARSHALL

DEDICATION

This book is dedicated to the men and women of Christian radio and television. You impact generations of fatherless children with the Father's message.

CONTENTS

Introduction

"Have a nice day;" "Good morning;" "Have a great one." These are all greetings and expressions we use casually with people. They're really just a congenial "wish" for the person's day; some said more sincerely than others, I'm sure. The Psalmist asks in chapter 34:12, "What man is he who desires life and longs for many days, that he may see good?" Basically, who wants to live a long life with all kinds of consecutive great days? Okay, now is the time for you to get all excited and shout out loud "I do!"

You already have great provision for the makings of one blessed day after another. You may disagree based on your present situation, but I've learned that God is true, and it's His Word against yours. Jesus talked about our entering into the Kingdom of God like a little child, if we are to enter in at all (Luke 18:17). Now to explain, God's Kingdom is His way of doing things and being right. So, stepping into God's great provision is likened to a child being helped and led by his father. Trust and confidence are the implicit virtues we expect when imagining this picture. However, some have been hurt by their earthly parents. That fogs their ability to interpret natural feelings and expectations.

There is no reason for a newborn child to face the challenge of reinventing the wheel or rediscovering a cure that is common to our medical world. Yet many children are born into this world with little to no true father's influence. They get a thick blast of pop culture, and they're driven by trends to find acceptance. Technology closes the world in around us, we can do anything and yet we can do nothing. We can do nothing to save ourselves from a meaningless existence. We need to know where we came from, otherwise each generation starts from scratch, desperately trying to find their purpose. A true father begets a child and therefore identity and purpose are no mystery; it's a direct flow from the relationship of origin. I know what it's like to try to do things only to realize again and again — I was basically trying to reinvent "the wheel." Though I didn't have a dad growing up, I did have a godly mother. She taught me that God would be a "Father to the fatherless," and that drove me to pursue His Word. After all, that is how a father imparts — by his word. Even punishment is a wasted experience unless understanding is imparted from father to child. Unless you know something to be true, it can have no effect on your life. You can fake it, but sooner or later you come away feeling deceived and ashamed.

Jesus was 12 years old when He went "solo" in Jerusalem while His parents were headed for home in Galilee (Luke 2:43-52). They thought He was with the caravan, and after going a day's journey, they discover that He's not there. For three anxious days they search until they find Jesus back in Jerusalem sitting among the religious leaders of the day, listening to them and asking questions. When Jesus hears how His parents had been looking for Him, He asks, "How is that you had to look for Me? Did you not know I must be about My Father's business?" Think about this: Jesus wonders at them searching for Him, because even though it's a big city, where else would He be but surrounded by wise people, learning? And even more incredible is the Lord learning from those He'll actually have to die to save. What humility!

So what is the Father's business anyway? Wisdom. People say, "I want to be like Jesus." Then you must be about your "Father's business," and it starts with wisdom. Look at Luke 2:52. It says that Jesus increased in Wisdom, and He increased in favor with God and with man. Just imagine the reality of God's own Son having to increase in wisdom and favor. Amazing! The actual ministry of Jesus started 18 years later and was an overflow of the progressive increase of those elements in Him. But let's not miss the relevance of how the gain of Wisdom applies to us. Proverbs says that it is the foundation. God used Wisdom to make everything that was ever made, including day and night. Consider that Jesus wasn't born preaching and teaching, but He grew to that place by Wisdom. The Bible says to "get it" — wisdom.

As we increase in wisdom, we increase in favor with God and with man. In Christ we already have all God's favor, but to walk in it we need to know how. It's the picture of an heir being subject to his or her own servants until maturity. The Father has willed the family fortune to you, but in His wisdom He has directed the servants to teach you the foundations of Kingdom principles until you graduate from level to level of competence. You can see that the benefits and opportunities will grow along with the responsibility.

Building anything worthwhile must have a foundation. Each day is meant to be a gift of time God entrusts to you. It is an unlimited blessing loaded with vast potential — this thing called time. The Father has not only provided for you but is willing to give investment counsel so that everyday brings you expected rewards. Buckle up and get ready to grab hold of the explosive power that has been hidden and dormant in your life for far too long. God's Word will transform you and your day with His abundant life. Enjoy.

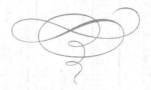

God's Way... Man's Way

BUILDING YOUR LIFE
ONE DAY AT A TIME

What do you want out of life? It's a very important question, because your pursuit is proof of what you desire. Those choices make you who you are. Simply put; what you want is who you are. Some people don't like that kind of math, but then a lot of people don't like who they are. Just like the units on a measuring tape help us grasp the size or length of something, God's Word is a straight edge that you can use to accurately measure your life against. That measurement is so precise that you can know where you're going in this life and the next by where you see yourself on the "line" of God's Word.

The Proverbs is one of my favorite books in the Bible. It's full of practical wisdom and teachings on the fine art of living. It is full of colorful characters from foolish, young men to exceptionally wise women; murderers and fools to inventors and kings. For anyone willing to stop and listen, it is a book full of wisdom that will help you make the most of each day.

From the moment you are born, life is all about your basic needs being met, your desires being fulfilled, and making the right choices. Even the bad stuff done to us will require a decision on our part that determines who we become. A life is built by making one turn and one choice at a time. Everything that is built must have a foundation. The quality of that foundation will not just determine the strength, but how the project will turn out.

Jesus used this as an example in Matthew 7:24, *"Everyone who hears these words of mine and does them, is like a wise man who built his house upon a rock."* The story goes on to say that violent storms came, but the house didn't budge because it was solidly established. Then Jesus says in verse 26, *"And everyone who hears these words of Mine and does not do them will be like a stupid man who built his house upon the sand."* The end of the story is another great storm and the total destruction of the foolish man's house. To perceive things as God does is the gift of wisdom — the measurement of God's Word in a person's life. Two men and each built a house. That's simply how the world would view this story. Wisdom, on the other hand, examines the foundations and says, "One man built a good house, and the other man wasted his money on a pile of rubble."

Wisdom knows what is to come. Proverbs 1:7 says, *"The reverent and worshipful fear of the Lord is the beginning and*

the principal part of knowledge; but fools despise skillful
and godly Wisdom, instruction and discipline." Wisdom
says you need to build on the rock. The fool says that it's
too much work and much easier to build on the sand. God
and His Word are one. Jesus is the "express image of God's
person" making Him the living Word and the perfect picture
of wisdom (Hebrews 1:3). Make it your prayer today to
build your life on the Rock, Christ Jesus. Remember that
Jesus always met people with one general question, "What
do you want?" Don't let your desires be shaped by your
experiences or culture because then you're just building
on the sand. Hebrews 12:2 says, *"Be transformed by the
renewing of your mind,"* and that happens as you read or
hear the Word of God and put It in to action in your life.

BIBLE FOCUS — PROVERBS 1:7

*"The reverent and worshipful fear of the Lord is the beginning
and the principal and choice part of knowledge [its starting
point and its essence]; but fools despise skillful and godly
Wisdom, instruction and discipline."* AMP

PRAY THE WORD

Lord, help me to never despise your wisdom, instruction,
or discipline. For all the times I have, forgive me. I choose
to reverence Your name and worship You. The knowledge
of You, Lord, is the foundation I want for my life. In Jesus'
Name, Amen.

What about my needs?
All I have is this key and this
can opener!!

You've Got It — Use It!

Since I was a kid, I have been playing music in bands and always involved in some kind of live performance. That adds up to a lot of dealings with sound technicians and the systems they run. Every situation is different, but a soundman (as even the girls are called) that understands music and the equipment is a performers dream come true. I've been in auditoriums where the equipment was state of the art, but the technician was lacking the personal tools to run the system. The end result was bad sound, feedback, and a lot of frustrated people. Having "the goods" sitting right in front of you but lacking the understanding and knowledge of how it works is considered undiscovered potential.

Let's look at it this way; a family lost at sea will starve to death with a boat full of canned goods, unless they have a can opener. You would have to have a key to get into a fortress. You would need a code to access a bank account. And let's be honest guys, most of the time we need directions to get to where we're going. Proverbs 2:1,2, and 5 says, *"My son (daughter), if you will receive my words, and hide my commandments with you; so that you incline your ear to wisdom, and apply your heart to understanding ... Then shall you understand the fear of the Lord, and find the knowledge of God."*

There are many people that have read the Ten Commandments and have even memorized some, or all, of them. It is obvious, though, from the fruit that grows out of their lives, that they have no understanding or knowledge of those truths. It is like an actor who has memorized a scientific formula for a movie he's in but has absolutely no idea how to apply it to his life. It's of no profit to him other than for role-playing. Sadly, this is the way God's Word is to many. But not you!

We are told in Proverbs that if we will receive God's words and "hide" His commandments in our hearts, we will understand and gain knowledge. This receiving of God's Word is not to be done in a casual, complacent attitude but a respectful embracing of It as if going after treasure (Proverbs 2:4). I like the word-picture we get in verse 2. Imagine it with me; a person bending their ear and leaning over to hear what Wisdom has to say. Do you hold God's Word in your heart like treasure, or is it just a traditional belief that you're content with? The Bible says, *"The traditions of men make the word of God of no effect."* Now that is scary. Let's violently get rid of every ungodly, weak notion designed to put God in a box. That can only happen when you grab onto God's truth and apply it to your heart. Today, grab the treasure (God's Word) in one hand, take the key (action) in the other, and bring them together. Now that's the making for a great day!!

BIBLE FOCUS — PROVERBS 2:1, 2, & 5

"My son (daughter), if you will receive my words, and hide my commandments with you; so that you incline your ear to wisdom, and apply your heart to understanding ... Then shall you understand the fear of the Lord, and find the knowledge of God." KJV

PRAY THE WORD

Heavenly Father, I am your child, so I dedicate the arena of my heart to receiving Your Word. As I purposely hide Your commandments in my heart, I know that I will have a supernatural inclination toward Your wisdom, and understanding will be mine. I need these keys so I can truly know You and see Your power actively working in my life. In Jesus' Name. Amen.

Hey you Guys, ever since Dale Got
his new GPS unit—he's Being led
to Green pastures & still waters.

GOD'S POSITIONING SATELLITE

A few years ago, some very dear friends surprised me with a gift. It was a personal navigation system, which is basically a hand held version of the GPS (Global Positioning Satellite) systems built into some cars. Living a lot of my life on the road and always having to be some place new, this was a great blessing. Now it didn't matter if I was in downtown San Francisco, the plains of Nebraska, or the narrow streets of Cape town, South Africa; I could see where I was going and how best to get there. I have a pretty good sense of direction, but I have trusted that sense in the past and have gotten totally lost. If you have ever been lost before, it can be frustrating, and depending on where you are, it can also make you really nervous. There is potential for a lot of anxiety when you are questioning your inner sense of direction too. Not being able to see the signposts in life you're looking for, and then various factors like "time" begin bearing down on you.

I was traveling through a snowstorm one day when up ahead the police were shutting down the highway and forcing everyone to take the exit. I found myself in a small town where the only two hotels in the area were already booked up. Worse yet, I was on a schedule and had to be some place on time. I flipped on my navigation system and could see that I was not far from a road that ran parallel to the freeway I was just forced off from. Even though it was almost impossible because of the storm to track myself on a conventional map, it was effortless with the GPS system. I remember how amazed I felt. Here I was traveling on unfamiliar back roads that had no visible names but doing it with total confidence. The heavy storm left me with little sense of direction, and, of course, anything I could see didn't look familiar anyway. Still, I had total peace about the direction I was taking.

Proverbs 3:5 instructs us to, *"Lean on, trust in, and be confident in the Lord with all your heart and mind and do not rely on your own insight or understanding"* (AMP). If you're traveling some place, you can't rely on the GPS system for five minutes and then turn it off for the next five and do your own thing. You're not going to get to your destination that way. Psalm 31 is a beautiful song about putting your trust in the Lord. In verse 3 it says, *"Lead me, and guide me."* The interesting thing about the GPS system is that the signal is always there, all over the world. The device in your car or hand is really just a receiver of the information transmitted from way above the earth — a satellite. I can be lost in downtown New York City, have my GPS navigator in my back pocket, good clear signal from outer space, and still stay lost. Unless I turn on my hand-held system and trust its information, I will wander in ignorance. Being lost is a terrible place to be. Isn't it funny, though, how you can be in the same geographical position but go from being lost to found instantly. Nothing seems to have changed outwardly, but the difference is what you know.

God has provided you and me with an internal GPS system that is constantly searching for Him. You know the way! People who know the way are bold, confident, and have a joy even in the middle of a storm. They don't walk by what they feel, but they're led and directed from above. God always wants to help you, and it's not His will for you to wander around in the dark. Jesus once said to a crowd of people, "He who has ears to hear, let him hear." Basically He was saying, "You've got a GPS system on the inside of you, and the signal is strong. Turn it on and go this way!" Trust the Lord today, because He is sending you strong direction and not willing that you should be lost.

BIBLE FOCUS — PROVERBS 3:5

"Lean on, trust in, and be confident in the Lord with all your heart and mind and do not rely on your own insight or understanding." AMP

PRAY THE WORD

Today I lean on and trust in You, Lord. Let the full weight of my confidence be in what You tell me, because You see and know everything. You love me and want to direct me, so I choose to consult with You for all my direction. In Jesus' Name. Amen.

So why didn't Tim come?
Are you kidding? He still
can't decide if earth is round
or flat.

PROMOTION COMES FROM GOD

K nowing the will of God is essential to doing the will of God. In the New Testament, Saul thought he was doing the will of God by murdering all the Christians he found, until he met Jesus on the road to Damascus (Acts 9). That day he asked the Son of God, "What do you want me to do?" (See verse 6.) Then Jesus told him. The real will of God was in total contrast to what Saul was already doing in God's name. He went from killing Christians known as Saul, to serving people named Paul and became one of the most well known apostles.

God's will and His Word are one and the same, just as God and His Word are one. Saul had a rich education in God's Word, but he was so blinded by the religious traditions of his culture, he honestly didn't know God's will. Jesus rebuked the religious leaders of His day calling them "blind guides" (Matthew 23:16). It's not very encouraging to think of your guide as blind, so let's go right to God's Word and see what it says to you. Proverbs 4:8 instructs, *"Prize Wisdom highly and exalt her, and she will exalt and promote you; she will bring you to honor when you embrace her."* Can this be true? Does God really want you to be promoted? In 1 Peter 5 God's Word says, *"Humble yourselves therefore under the mighty hand of God, that He may exalt you in due time."* These truths of God are both encouraging and convicting. When you know the will of God, you have a picture of who you are in Him and all He has provided for you. The convicting part is when you see the reality of who you are without Him and how "out to lunch" you've been.

Maybe you've secretly desired to have a position of honor or a big promotion, but you feel that wouldn't be very "spiritual" and definitely not in God's plan. Hey! We just heard the will of God for your life —wisdom exalting and promoting you, and God lifting you up. The office of "President of the United States" is an honorable position among men, and I pray that there are some godly people who embrace Wisdom and desire to be the President. The last thing the devil wants is for you as a child of God to know the perfect will of God. He can't stop you except that he keeps you ignorant of the truth and in the dark. If people don't know and understand God's will to save them from their sin, they remain in their sin.

Before the 1400s most people thought the world was flat. Submitting to that knowledge may have been the popular thing of that day, but it wasn't true. In the 1950s most people believed that a man could never walk on the moon, but that didn't make it true. No matter what the world may say, ignorance is *not* bliss, and there are *no* points in God's Kingdom for not knowing what He wants you to know. If you don't know God has saved you, you cannot be saved. If you don't know that God wants to promote you, you cannot receive His promotion. When you are given a gift, it can only be used once you actually receive it. God said in Hosea 4:6, *"My people are destroyed for lack of knowledge."* Knowledge of what? The knowledge of His will for your life. Your job today is to exalt Wisdom and believe God's Word. It doesn't matter who says you can't walk on the moon, you know that promotion comes from God (Psalm 75:6). Using His knowledge and wisdom will promote you and your day far beyond anything you could ever imagine.

BIBLE FOCUS — PROVERBS 4:8
"Prize Wisdom highly and exalt her, and she will exalt and promote you; she will bring you to honor when you embrace her." AMP

PRAY THE WORD
Thank you, Father God, for Wisdom. You used Wisdom to make everything that was made, and now You give me this precious gift. I know by Your Word that promotion is for me, so I prize the gift of Wisdom. Show me today how I can embrace and exalt your Word. In Jesus' Name. Amen.

EASY IS NOT SO EASY

Y ou're walking along and suddenly you hear the voice of God; "Let your way in life be far from her, and come not near the door of her house (avoid the very scenes of temptation)." Who is God talking about? I mean if God told you to avoid someone like the plague, it would be a good thing to know exactly who that person was. Another good question is why would God want us to stay away from anyone to the extreme that we're to even avoid their house?

First of all let's remind ourselves of God's character. God is good, and God is love. John 3:16 says, *"God so loved the world that He gave His only begotten Son, that whoever believes in Him shall not perish but everlasting life."* When God warns you to not do something, or not go somewhere, it's because He loves you and wants you to live a long, healthy, fruitful life. Looking at verses 9-14 of Proverbs 5, we see what happens if you go near this person we're warned about: you'll give your honor to others, give your years to those without mercy, give your wealth away, give your strength away, you'll groan when your end comes, you'll hate all wisdom and basically die miserable. Ouch! That is a picture of everything God does not want to have happen to you. The truth is that God wants you blessed. If God would sacrifice His own Son for you, how much more will He give you when you turn your life over to Him?

The devil wants you to have a wrong picture of God. He wants you to see God as mean and looking to keep you from all the good stuff in life. This could not be further from the truth. The Bible says that every good and perfect gift comes down from the Father of Lights. That's God! Psalm 35:27 says that God has pleasure in the prosperity of His servant. And if He wants His servants to be prosperous, just think how much more He will give His children!

So let's get back to the voice of God that has just transformed your life with this bold warning. I mean He's just told you to avoid someone. Who? In Proverbs 5:3 we're told it's a "loose" woman. The whole chapter starts off addressed to, "My Son." This isn't about gender, so if you're God's daughter, you can consider this person a seductive, immoral man too. Now, you may have already been "bit" and are suffering some of the consequences of such an association. It's not too late. You may have even seen *yourself* as the person that God has warned His children against. God has an awesome plan for your life. It starts with coming to Jesus and asking Him to save you. He'll make you a brand new person, nothing like what you used to be. Jesus delivered a prostitute, and she became one of the most talked about godly women of the Bible. That doesn't change the fact that there were other people in Jesus' day that refused the path of life and preferred darkness. Today is no different. We're told to exercise proper discretion, and we just heard God's Word — walk in the path of life today. That means there are some places you need to just plain avoid. That is faith, because it's believing God and believing that He has put you on the path of an unbelievably good life.

BIBLE FOCUS — PROVERBS 5:8

"Let your way in life be far from her, and come not near the door of her house [avoid the very scenes of temptation]." AMP

PRAY THE WORD

God, I ask You to keep my way far from people who would lead me to death. Give me discernment to know which places to stay away from, and help me avoid the very pictures of temptation. I choose life. In Jesus' Name. Amen.

I thank thee God that I
don't play guitar like that
wretched fellow over
yonder.

SEX, DRUGS AND ROCK N' ROLL

You can tell a lot about someone by the things they love. The same is true if you know what they hate. Now there's a big difference between tolerating something and hating it. Most people tolerate things in their life that they dislike, but the intensity of hate expresses a zero tolerance. This thing — hate — has got a bad rap because of its total misuse by people. You should know that there are things God hates. That's right! Proverbs 6:16 says, *"These six things does the Lord hate."* Notice that there are certain things that God hates, not people, but things. God loves you. God loves all people. We know that He is angry with the wicked, but then my Mom was angry with me when I was doing stupid things too. She still loved me, though. So many people live life feeling like God hates them, and it's no wonder. He gets so much bad press from ignorant people.

Let's go right to the Word and find out what God hates. Verse 17 kicks off the list: *"A proud look, a lying tongue, hands that shed innocent blood, a heart that devises wicked imaginations, feet that are swift in running to mischief, a false witness that speaks lies."* God hates this stuff. He doesn't tolerate it or just strongly dislikes It. He hates it! Most of you grew up thinking God hated sex, drugs, and rock 'n roll!

Notice the first thing in the list is "a proud look". The Bible makes it clear in many places that pride and arrogance are always a prelude to destruction. Usually a proud look goes along with an attitude of being superior to those around you. Jesus told a story about two men in a temple talking to God (Luke 18:10-14). The one said, "Thank God I'm not like that guy over there, a sinner." The other guy said, "God be merciful to me a sinner." Jesus concluded that the humble man went to his home justified before God while the proud man went home still in his sin. God hates pride. It keeps you blind to the truth and locked in the disease of your sin.

To a Father that wants His children blessed, pride is a hateful enemy. Just like these other things God hates, they're all meant for your destruction. Satan likes for people to get side tracked with religiously tainted rules and prejudice. That way, just like the Pharisee in Luke 18, they remain ignorant of the sin that's destroying their life. Do not put words in God's mouth, but rather, put His Word in your mouth.

God hates covenant breaking, not sex. Sex is God's design for blessing *within marriage*. The Bible says in 3 John 2, *"I wish above all things that you would prosper and be in health, even as your soul prospers."* That means if a legal drug administered by a physician can benefit your health, good. But if you're trying to escape reality with drugs, watching soap operas, or eating too much, then you're living a lie and falling prey to twisted imaginations. God said He hates *a lying tongue and a heart that devises wicked imaginations.* Remember, do not put words in God's mouth, but say what He says. Don't debate over terms like "Rock n' roll", but focus on the truth. Music is a gift from God, and He has instructed us to use it for worship, for war, and as a joyful noise. Play it loud, or play it soft, for celebration and for comfort. God hates sin (1 Samuel 15:23) but He loves the sinner, and He loves you.

God hates stuff that interferes with you being blessed because His "wish" is for you to prosper in every area of your life. To stay far away from what God hates is to make more room for love. Watch and see how love will explode in your life as you make zero room for anything God calls evil.

BIBLE FOCUS — PROVERBS 6:16,17,18

"These six things does the Lord hate ... A proud look, a lying tongue, hands that shed innocent blood, a heart that devises wicked plans, feet that are swift in running to evil, a false witness who speaks lies ..." NKJV

PRAY THE WORD

Father, I acknowledge that You are God and You are Love. It makes perfect sense that You would hate the things that hurt and destroy the ones You love. Help me to stay far from pride, lies, murder, evil images and schemes, the delight of making trouble, and the perversion of an opportunity to speak truth. I desire to walk in love, so in the Name of Jesus, let there be zero tolerance of these things in my life. Amen.

A Little Sister Talk

When I was eight years old, Dad left me, my Mom, and my younger brother and sister. Some painful things had gone on in his life and he had turned to all kinds of "fixes" to ease the pain. Those "fixes" were destroying his life and leading him far away from anyone who loved him. A father has an awesome call on his life in the family, and so, when he vacates the position, there can be a terrible void left behind. Take a look at this fatherless generation and just see what has happened.

My Mom was always faithful to remind us that God is a Father to the fatherless. You see; God wants you to have a strong sense of family. That's why God sowed His Son Jesus; to gain a whole family with you right next to Him. The Bible says, *"God sets the lonely in families"* (Psalm

68:6 NIV). It's not God's will for you to feel like you don't belong but, rather, that you have a strong sense of identity and family. I've not grown up with a sense of loss in my life because God has truly been a Father to me. He has encouraged me to lean on and trust in Him. God has been my defense and refuge at all times. There's nothing like knowing that your Dad is bigger and stronger than everyone else's.

Here is another wonderful side of God I have discovered over the years of having Him look after me; His Wisdom. In Proverbs 7:4 God instructs us, *"Say to Wisdom, You are my sister; and call understanding your cousin."* You may have come from a loving family or one of the most abusive situations imaginable, but you have the family of your dreams in Jesus. John 1:12 tells us that, *"as many as received [Jesus], to them He gave power to become the sons of God, even to them that believe on His name."* You have a new spiritual family name, and Wisdom is your sister.

I've been blessed with a great sister and brother in my natural family. My sister is non-judgmental and very generous. She is easily concerned about me, loves to know what I'm up to and would help me in a heartbeat. Far better though, you and I have the same family member in Wisdom. God's says to call her your sister and we have a cousin named Understanding. There's no need for us to be alone another day.

Open up your heart this moment and speak Proverbs 7:4; *"Wisdom, you are my sister and understanding, you are my cousin. I love you and want your help. I'm not alone but I have the most amazing family in Jesus' Name."* You can't walk with family like that and not expect to be blessed. Deuteronomy 28:2 says, *"All these blessings shall come on you, and overtake you, if you diligently listen to the voice of the Lord your God."* God's voice is Wisdom. Can you see it? You're walking with Wisdom and now you're being chased by blessings that are going to overtake you. That means they're going to find you! You don't even have to try to be blessed today, just walk with your heavenly family.

BIBLE FOCUS — PROVERBS 7:4

"Say to Wisdom, You are my sister; and call understanding your nearest kin." NKJV

PRAY THE WORD

According to the Word of God I say, Wisdom is my sister and Understanding is my cousin. I have an amazing family in Christ who celebrates my life. I choose to diligently listen as the Holy Spirit of God coordinates these mentors in my life. Thank you, Father, for Wisdom and Understanding. In Jesus' Name. Amen.

Go ahead ... make your day!

GO AHEAD — MAKE YOUR DAY

Proverbs 8 has to be one of my favorite chapters in the Bible because it covers everything from the time before creation to the promise of life and favor with God. This chapter never fails to inspire a sense of awe in my heart. Listen to what God says as the voice of Wisdom in verse 17. *"I love them that love me; and those that seek me early shall find me."* This is quite a promise, especially if you consider it in the context of this whole chapter. From verse 22 to 31, we find out that God has possessed Wisdom from before the creation of the world and used Wisdom to make everything that was made. Wisdom was there.

Genesis 1 says that everything God made He spoke it into being. Those had to have been some seriously wisdom-filled words! And now you and I are given the invitation to use this same awesome force to speak life into each and everyone of our days. One thing I find provoking is that Wisdom loves those who love her. Those who hate Wisdom love death. That's quite a contrast in destiny. It reminds me of when God said to the children of Israel, *"Today I've set before you life and death; choose life"* (Deuteronomy 30:15). You may be like a lot of people, afraid to make any choices because you're afraid to make the wrong one. Start today and choose to love Wisdom. Verse 7 promises that Wisdom will only speak truth and it'll be worth more than rubies (verse 11).

There are a lot of people who make decisions and then cry later saying, "Why doesn't God help me? Doesn't He care?" We heard in verse 17, *"those that seek me early shall find me."* It doesn't work when we make our own decisions based on our own limited knowledge and then ask God to bless it after the fact. God prospers those who seek His will and His wisdom. Don't get in the trap of making your plans independent of God and then only seeking Him for damage control. Seek Wisdom now, early, before you take another step.

Look at the results of getting wisdom. There is strength, counsel, discovery of inventions, and understanding (just to name a few). How many times have you heard people in an exasperated tone say, "If I could only understand." It is a tired, old saying of many good intentioned people that we'll understand it "in the sweet by and by". Well, if every doctor throughout history had been content to say, "Hey, this is just the way it is," then people would still be dying of simple infections because penicillin would never have been invented.

The truth is we don't like taking responsibility for the bad things in life. One of the most convicting truths hit me in this chapter of Proverbs when I read verse 18, *"Riches and honor are with me (Wisdom)."* It didn't take me long to realize that there was strong evidence that I had been ignoring the companionship of Wisdom. The great thing about the truth is that it convicts and encourages. When Wisdom reproves you, it redirects your steps from failure to success. God makes the day, each and everyday. Now *you* make your day by declaring your love for God's wisdom and diligently seeking it early.

BIBLE FOCUS — PROVERBS 8:17

"I love them that love me; and those that seek me early shall find me." KJV

PRAY THE WORD

God, I realize more and more that wisdom is in You. I love wisdom and I know wisdom loves me. I am determined to consult with You, Father, before making decisions, and I know that You will give me wisdom. In Jesus' Name. Amen.

NON-SCORNING SECTION

You turn on the television or the radio and it's there. Sitting in a coffee shop or a mall, you can hear it with ease. Kids practice it at school, and parents use it at home. People in politics and others in authority do it all the time. It's the fine art of scorning. To scorn is to openly disrespect and show extreme contempt for something or someone.

Scorn has bit at many preachers, saints and sinners. You see, scorn can never be justified by its victim. What I mean is, no matter how guilty the person really is, there is never a time when it's right to scorn. Psalm 1 opens up with this warning. *"Blessed is the man who walks not in the counsel of the ungodly, or stands in the way of sinners, or sits in the seat of the scornful."* You want to be blessed don't you? Get up off that seat, and watch your mouth!

Here is an interesting slant on the subject that I want you to see when examining yourself. Proverbs 9:8 says, *"Reprove not a scorner, lest he hate you; reprove a wise man, and he will love you."* The word "reproof" sounds bad to a lot of people, but the truth is, it's a beautiful thing. When some hear reproof is coming, they arm themselves with excuses and every counter-attack they can come up with. God is telling us in Proverbs not to reprove a scorner because he'll hate you, but if you give the same thing to a wise man, he'll love you. When I read that, I wanted to know more about this thing called reproof. If giving something to a wise man makes him love you, chances are that "thing" is very valuable.

I looked up the word "reprove" to find its original meaning. It comes from the Hebrew root "to be right," causing the recipient to have the decision or be justified. The word includes the meaning of being corrected, convinced, and reasoned with, even to the point of being chastened. Contrary to our carnal natures' instinct, reproof is not about us being wrong, but more importantly about God's desire to make us right! Isn't that amazing? We can see from this verse that reproof is a valuable thing that does not belong to the scorner but to the wise. In fact, if you read the verses that come before, we're told to "forsake the foolish" and get ready for lots of abuse if we reprove the wrong people.

I don't like the idea of being passed over when God is revealing secrets for life or Holy Ghost information that will put me at the right place at the right time. The Psalmist asked, "What man is he who desires life and longs for many days, that he may see good?" (Psalm 34:12) Do you want to know how to have a whole lot of great days in a row with all kinds of blessings in every one of them? The answer comes to us in the next line saying, *"keep your tongue from evil and your lips from speaking deceit."* When you scorn, you interpret something with your tongue to openly mock someone. No matter how factual the words are, the tone and intent of your heart is deceitful. It will blind you and disqualify you from the blessings that belong to the wise. Ask the Lord for help and starting right now. When you commit your mouth to the glory of God, there is no room for scorn. Remember Psalm 1, scorning may seem as comfortable to you as a cozy couch, but blessed are those who stay out of that seat.

BIBLE FOCUS — PROVERBS 9:8
"Reprove not a scorner, lest he hate you; reprove a wise man, and he will love you". NKJ

PRAY THE WORD
God, I don't want to be a scorner, but I want to be wise. Help me to recognize reproof and the difference between it and abuse. Keep me from the error of trying to give something valuable to someone who really doesn't want it. In Jesus' Name. Amen.

Chapter Ten

REWARD CONSCIOUS

When I was a boy, I would often spend the summers at my grandparent's home on the east coast. They had a place out in the country and right on the ocean. There were always lots of gardens around and crops of all kinds. One of my favorite things to do toward the end of the summer was to work in the fields bringing in the hay. It was just feed for the livestock, but it was fun. Bringing in a harvest should be a time of celebration. A harvest always has a purpose and a sense of increase.

When we would walk through my grandfather's garden, we expected to see more than what we originally planted. Seeds were planted sometime in the spring, and then throughout the summer we would keep coming back to the garden looking for the increase. What would you think if I told you we would plant seeds in the springtime and then just forget about the harvest? Or maybe we just never went back at harvest time because we trusted God and didn't think it was right to expect anything? I'm sure you would consider that ridiculous or at least very misguided. Proverbs 10:5 says, *"He who gathers in summer is a wise son, but he who sleeps in harvest is a son who causes shame."*

Gathering up a harvest is considered a wise thing to do in God's book. Neglecting a harvest is shameful. There have been some hard times in history when harvest time came and there were no crops. There might have been a drought or too much rain, but either way, the crops failed. The 1930s saw a lot of failed crops, so much so that they called them the "dirty thirties". Crops just never came up. The poverty that came out of those times for a lot of people was harsh. No harvest meant hunger, lost homes, desperation, and many broken families losing touch with each other in the efforts to survive. Even today a lost or neglected harvest will always translate into an open door for shame. God does not want that for you. Read the last half of Deuteronomy 28, and you'll see that a failed harvest is part of the curse. It's not God's will for you to live your life in a curse. That is the reason that Jesus came to set you free.

Hebrews 11:6 makes this statement, *"Without faith it is impossible to please God: for he that comes to God must believe that He is, and that He is a rewarder of them that diligently seek Him."* Harvest is a reward and God is the Rewarder. It only works, however, if you come to God, believe in Him and that He wants to reward you.. Remember what God says, *"He who gathers in summer is a wise son."* You may know very little about farming, but in God's Kingdom you are called to be diligent about your fields. You didn't know you had fields? Oh yes! Your own heart is a vast planting ground that can bring you a rich harvest. In Luke 8 Jesus tells the parable of the sower and the seed. In verse 11 He reveals that the seed is the Word of God, and as you read on you can see that the ground is your heart. Matthew 12:35 says that a good man brings good things out of the treasure of his heart where an evil man brings evil things out of his heart. What kinds of things are coming out of your heart?

You have a very real enemy who doesn't want you to have a good harvest. He doesn't want you to experience God's reward, because it's full of life and power. In Luke 8:12 it says that the devil steals the Word out of your heart so that you will not believe what It says. Here we are back to believing God, the real core to faith; which is the backbone of harvesting. You can just sleep through harvest, but I know that if you are diligent to believe, you'll reap the rewards of being a wise child of God. Today your eyes are opened to vast fields that are yours to possess. Now is the time to be harvest minded. Yes, now is the time to be blessed so you can be a blessing to others.

BIBLE FOCUS — PROVERBS 10:5
"He who gathers in summer is a wise son; but he who sleeps in harvest is a son who causes shame." NKJV

PRAY THE WORD
Jesus, you taught us to be conscious of sowing and reaping. God, help me to act in faith and be a child of Yours that reaps in the right seasons. You are the Rewarder, so help me to be diligent in my attitudes and expectations. You are faithful, so help me to be faithful to discern and harvest every field in my life. In Jesus' Name. Amen.

Whew! It's Been all after-
noon! How long do I have
to wait anyway?

GET A FUTURE

To the south of Toronto, Canada, is Niagara Falls. That whole area is called the Niagara Peninsula, and it is known to be some of the most fertile land in North America. There are vineyards everywhere, and the fall is always heavy with the aroma of grapes. Of course, there are other types of crops grown there such as corn, cherries, apples, and the list goes on. I know a little bit about this place, because it was my home for the better part of growing up. The thing I want to bring to your attention is, although the ground was basically the same, I watched as year after year there grew an incredible variety of crops. As you can imagine, those different crops brought in quite a varied profit from one crop to the other.

The Bible says clearly that God is no respecter of persons, and yet every life is so different in its final measure. God tells us that He loves the world, but you see many people go through life with no evidence of love in it. Why would

this be? Let me point you to this truth in Proverbs 11:17.
*"The merciful, kind and generous man benefits himself [for
his deeds return to bless him], but he who is cruel and
callous [to the wants of others] brings on himself retribution."*
In this context, a person's deeds become "seeds" that return
to them a harvest like what they planted in others.

I've seen, even among Christians, a wide span of crops.
We just heard from Proverbs that there are different seeds
(deeds) that a person can sow into the lives of others.
There is good seed for a good harvest and bad seed for
a bad harvest. Seeds of kindness bring in a harvest that
benefits the one who sows it. Your "deeds" can be working
for you, bringing in a return harvest full of blessing. Jesus
said, *"Don't be deceived for God is not mocked; whatever
a man sows, that also shall he reap."* Your future is being
decided today with the seeds you sow. Your words are
seeds, and your choices are seeds. We were just told that
mercy and generosity are seeds, but so is cruelty.

No one has ever planted corn and gotten a harvest of
apples. The seed doesn't discriminate against the sower; it
is what it is. A common mistake people make is to spend
their energy looking for someone to blame for the "junk" in
their life. Bad things happen in this world, but did you know
that forgiveness is an incredible seed? I've seen people
sow this beautiful seed and watched as the most incredible
harvest grew up all around them. "It's too hard to forgive,"
you may say, but the harvest of bitterness is cruel at best.
Remember that God said He would "give seed to the sower
and multiply the seed sown." He'll do it for you!

You are a sower, so ask God for that seed that may seem
impossible to you. Don't forget the process. The Word says
that it's "seed, time, and harvest." A blade may have come

out of the ground, but don't despise that small beginning. Even the beginnings of a mighty oak tree start quietly under the ground. So whatever you do, don't go digging it up because of impatience. Galatians 6:9 encourages us, "And let us not lose heart and grow weary and faint in well doing, for in due time we shall reap, if we do not faint."

When someone plants a seed, they are looking for a specific harvest so you must know what it is that you want. It's essential to sowing the right seeds. What kind of harvest are you looking for? Decide your future and choose your seed. Jesus wouldn't have died if your choices didn't matter. The ultimate seed you sow in this life is to confess with your mouth and believe in your heart that God raised Jesus from the dead, and "you shall be saved" (Romans 10:9). If it's by this seed of faith that you receive the greatest harvest, then *do not* neglect God's way of doing things, and get serious about wisdom. Set your eyes today on the "sure reward" of Proverbs 11:18, and go for it.

BIBLE FOCUS — PROVERBS 11:17
"The merciful, kind and generous man benefits himself [for his deeds return to bless him], but he who is cruel and callous [to the wants of others] brings on himself retribution." AMP

PRAY THE WORD
Father God, help me to sow the right kinds of seed in this life. Christ lives in me so I already have the power to be merciful, kind, and generous. I want to be blessed in every area of my life, and I realize that it all starts with planting the seeds You've already provided. Direct my sowing so that the harvest is big and You are honored. In Jesus' Name. Amen.

Boss Your Soul Happy!

"**A**nxiety in a man's heart weighs it down, but an encouraging word makes it glad" (Proverbs 12:25). Is there anything in your life weighing you down right now? Maybe you're worried about something, and it's like a black cloud hanging over your head. No matter where you go or what you do, you feel totally weighed down by your circumstances. When you look up the word "anxiety" in the dictionary, you'll find definitions such as: a painful uneasiness of mind over an impending ill; fearful concern; an abnormal sense of fear often marked by physiological signs. Sounds downright nasty!

Maybe you've heard the story of a guy in the Old Testament called Nabal who basically died of anxiety. His wife Abigail told him one morning how close he came to being killed because of his arrogance to the upcoming king, David (1

Samuel 25). The Bible says his heart "died within him, and he became as a stone." Isn't that amazing? The guy had never even seen David or his army, he just heard from his wife how close he came to getting his life destroyed and died anyway. Some people have dreams where they try to run away from something, but they're paralyzed with fear. Others actually live in a world where they are in that paralyzed grip, crippled, and numb from the inescapable doom bearing down on them. Just as with Nabal, the threat may no longer exist, but to the person whose mind is overwhelmed, the reality of that panic is still chasing them down.

The backbone of anxiety is fear, and that is one of the biggest enemies of all time. The Word of God says that "fear brings torment" (1 John 4:18). The number one killer in North America is heart disease. Studies and statistics give stress a high rating in cases attributed to this heart stopper. You can call it worry, fretting, being anxious, stressing, caring too much, or just plain fear; either way, it's deadly. When I was a boy I remember lying in bed worrying and not being able to sleep. My Mom was raising us kids alone, so I was worried about the rent money, worried about what people thought of us, worried I was stupid, and then worried I'd never fall asleep. Who says being eight doesn't have its problems? To live in torment of what may or may not happen is a cursed existence.

From the first page of the Bible to the last, God commands us to "Fear not." It's a command, *not* a suggestion. Still there are those who truly believe that it's being responsible to be loaded with care. Read all of Matthew 6. Over and over Jesus says, *"Take no thought"* when referring to the cares of life, but instead we're to *"seek first the kingdom of*

God, and His righteousness" (verse 33). 1 Peter 5:7 says, *"Casting all your care upon Him; for He cares for you."*

Good always overcomes evil, and light always defeats the dark. An idle mind is not the solution to a heart trained in rehearsing fear. Let's remember the last half of Proverbs 12:25, *"An encouraging word"* will make your heart *"glad."* There is no word so powerful and full of life as the Word of God. Aggressively defeat fear and worry with God's Word. Fight fear with a promise that has come from the lips of God. Jesus always answered Satan with, *"It is written"* and not some defensive, weak notion based on man's perception. This is your life we're talking about, so open up your mouth and *"let the redeemed of the Lord say so"* (Psalm 107:2). David the Psalmist would literally tell his soul, *"Bless the Lord, oh my soul; and all that is within me."* It's time for you to start bossing your heart and mind around with some encouraging words. If David did it, you need to do it.

BIBLE FOCUS — PROVERBS 12:25

"Anxiety in a man's heart weighs it down, but an encouraging word makes it glad." AMP

PRAY THE WORD

God, I don't want to live in a state of fear or anxiety, so right now I cast all my cares over onto You. You can make more sense of my life in 5 seconds than I can in the next 50 years. Help me to hold tight to Your life-giving Word and the encouraging things that You inspire others to say to me. You make my heart glad, and I praise You. In the Name of Jesus. Amen.

But are we being fair in
saying that this is an apple
tree? Yes, how do we know
its heart?

CAN'T WE ALL JUST BE FRIENDS?

eing politically correct is a pretty "hip" thing in this new millennium. There is a real push for tolerance, acceptance and, of course, being non-judgmental is paramount. Oh yeah, the Christians are in on it too. In fact, since I was a little boy I've heard people quote, *"Judge not, that you be not judged"* (Matthew 7:1). That *sounds* great and you can almost feel the global group hug coming on except, God's truth is not in political correctness.

The word "judge" here in Matthew 7:1 comes from the Greek word "krino" which means to distinguish or decide mentally. It goes further, though, and says, "to decide so that you can condemn and punish." You and I have not been called to be the judge, jury, and executioner, but you are called to distinguish in your mind. Before you start shaking your head, read John 7:24. *"Judge not according to the appearance, but judge righteous judgment."* Let me put it this way; God has called you to take a right measurement and according to His laws, make a distinction regarding the rightness of things, events, entertainment, politics, ethics, and yes, people.

Proverbs 13:20 counsels the child of God, *"He who walks with wise men shall be wise, but he who associates with fools shall be destroyed."* If you are at all interested in the benefits of being wise, or at least don't want to be destroyed, this verse from God's Word is a code to live by. There is no way of implementing it, though, without making a judgment. We're told to find wise people to be friends with and purposely cut off associations with fools.

God keeps accurate measurements of everyone from fools to kings in His Word. You don't have to drill to the center of an apple tree to know what kind of tree it is; just check out the fruit. This is a hard line for a lot of people because they don't like to believe that they're becoming the people they're hanging out with. They even use lines like, "Well, Jesus was a friend to the sinner." That is a line taken out of context from Matthew 11:19 when Jesus was correcting some ignorant folks saying, *"You call me a glutton, a drunk, and a friend of sinners."* Yes, Jesus loved the sinner. We've all sinned. He died for all of us, but Jesus didn't "hang out" with sinners. He met them at the crossroad of their life, forgave them, healed them, and said, *"Go and sin no more.* They weren't prostitutes or dishonest tax collectors anymore; they were daughters and sons of God. Think about this; the father of the prodigal son didn't lay down with his boy in the pigpen. 1 Corinthians 15:33 says, *"Do not be deceived! Bad company corrupts good morals and character."* It's a spiritual law that you become like whoever you hang out with. If you think that dating a fool will make *them* a better person and pull them *up* to your level, remember that they have the carnal law of "gravity" on their side.

How many of you loving parents would hire a known pedophile to baby-sit your children? Are you making a judgment? Yes, you sure are. It's not your place to condemn or punish this individual, but before God you have a *mandatory responsibility* to judge right from wrong. God have mercy on you if you don't. Making a distinction based on rightness is an act of love. Don't let the pendulum swing on this truth but keep it tight to God's Word. Guard your mouth from speaking evil against anyone, but choose to walk with the wise. You will be making the right choice for your day and choosing a much higher destiny.

BIBLE FOCUS — PROVERBS 13:20
"He who walks with the wise shall be wise, but he who associates with fools shall be destroyed." Combination of AMP & NKJ

PRAY THE WORD
Heavenly Father, I desire to be wise, and I know from Your Word that I need to associate with wise people. Help me to discern in my heart who I should walk with and those who don't qualify for my association. I cannot put my head in the sand over this touchy issue, because it's life or death. I choose life. Help me to always walk in love and be discerning, never condemning of another but never blinded by this world's version of ethics. I ask these things in the Name of Jesus. Amen.

THE TRUST FACTOR

Finding a place where you belong has been the search of people since the beginning of time. It's more than just a sense of belonging. To be protected and provided for are two other top needs we all share. In the Old Testament God told Abraham to leave his community and his country so that the Lord could show him a new homeland (Genesis 12:1). We can miss comprehending how difficult that must have been because we know for a fact that Abraham did it. We focus on the promises God made him such as; to make him a father of a great nation, bless him, make his name great, and make him a blessing to the world. There is an awesome principal that God is showing us here. Your position directly relates to the blessings you will receive from God.

When I say "position" I'm not just talking about geographical. It could mean letting go of some relationships, just as Abraham did, or it may be some kind of traditional thinking. Maybe you're holding on to the past, and the future remains out of reach. It really is a matter of owning an internal attitude that is convinced that God is Who He says He is. Proverbs 14:26 says, *"In the fear of the Lord is strong confidence; and his children shall have a place of refuge."* It's kind of funny in our day and age to associate "fear" with anything like "strong confidence" or "a place of refuge". That's because the fear of God is nothing like the worldly type of fear that we're told in the Bible to throw out. The fear of God is not only the beginning of Wisdom (Proverbs 1:7) and the hating of evil (Proverbs 8:13), but it is a satisfying fountain of life (14:27) and an actual place — a refuge.

Everybody needs a refuge; a hiding place where you are not only safe, but also a place where you can walk in strong confidence. Has anybody ever asked you, "Hey, where do you live?" Then you give them your address and maybe some directions. In this life, there are cities where even a fortified castle wouldn't be enough to keep you safe. Enemies can attack you from within your body, your family, and your mind. The *"reverent and worshipful fear of the Lord,"* as the Amplified Bible puts it, is this place you can reside in as you esteem God's Word above every other word, sense, and inclination.

Isaiah 1:19 says, *"If you are willing and obedient, you shall eat the good of the land."* What an awesome promise that is full of reward, so why are we so unwilling and afraid to obey? It's what I think of as the "trust factor". You cannot trust someone you don't know, and knowing God is the beginning of "the fear of God". The fear of the Lord I am speaking of is a healthy reverence for God Himself. There are those who shake their fist at God and curse

Him because they don't know Him. Even Christians in their ignorance credit God with things that are not at all in His character and then make the blanket statement, "It must have been the will of God." That is a direct offense to the Lord. The mercies of God are new every morning (Lamentations 3:22 & 23), and God's will is that none should perish. The tragedy is that many don't know they've been provided a fortress of safety in Him; then others willingly wander from His safety. At the very least, let's not dare credit God with the outcome. We have a life in Christ that is a place filled with strong confidence. God is who He is, regardless of what anyone thinks or says. The deciding factor in your life is your recognition and acceptance of Him. The discovery of God and His character is a land flowing with every blessing imaginable.

BIBLE FOCUS — PROVERBS 14:26

"In the fear of the Lord is strong confidence; and his children shall have a place of refuge." KJV

PRAY THE WORD

God, I believe that your Son Jesus died for my sins and that You raised Him up from the grave. Because of His blood, I've been made a child of Yours, Father. Help me to recognize Your provision and protection in my life. My desire is to increase in my knowledge of You and to grow in confidence as Your child. You have made a place for me, a place of refuge. Show me the spiritual process I must go through while being a child of Yours and walking on this earth. In Jesus' Name. Amen.

I tell you ... men can't fly ...
it's impossiBllllllllleeeee!!

FOR OR AGAINST YOU —
IT'S YOUR MOUTH

f you have watched any television at all, you've probably
seen some criminal having his rights read to him after
being arrested. "You have the right to remain silent,
anything you say can, and will, be used against you in a
court of law," is how part of it goes. Then there's the part
where a person is actually in court as a witness and they
make them put their hand on the Bible and swear to tell
the whole truth. What is all of that about? In the courts
of law, your words are evidence. That's right, it can be
the difference between being declared guilty or innocent.
Dishonest people many times have gone to great lengths to
buy someone's testimony; have a witness lie on the stand
or even have that witness killed if their testimony would
harm the case.

In this natural world, words spoken are a powerful thing, but when considered in the spiritual world, people often neglect their incredible force. As legal as words are in this natural world, they are far more potent on a spiritual plain. Remember that we are made in God's image. How did God make everything that was made? By *the Word of His mouth* He made everything. Matthew 12:36 say's that on the Day of Judgment, each person shall give an account of "every idle word" they speak. Here is the punch line, though: *"For by your words you shall be justified, and by your words you shall be condemned"* (verse 37). If you don't believe that every single word coming out of your mouth is the essence of your life, you're believing a huge lie and building a very sad tomorrow.

Your very salvation is dependent on your mouth. Romans 10:8 explains how the rightness of faith actually shows up in your life; it says, *"The Word is near you, even in your mouth."* As you read on you see in verse 9 that *"if you confess (that word of faith) with your mouth the Lord Jesus... you shall be saved."* Now, it is interesting that some people have no trouble believing their confession will profoundly effect their eternal outcome, but on the other hand, they think their confession has little to no effect here on earth.

Proverbs 15:4 says, *"A wholesome tongue is a tree of life; but perverseness in it is a breach in the spirit."* It's hard to imagine your tongue having that much power, but it's part of the way you were designed. I don't think any verse sums it up so plainly as Proverbs 18:21, *"Death and life are in the power of the tongue."* Wow! When you realize the absolute truth of this verse, you can't help but do a mental accounting of all the things you have been saying. Fallen human nature tends to affirm what it sees, hears, and feels.

Thank God that the Wright brothers didn't walk around saying, "People can't fly. It's never been done." They would have been stating the facts, but the facts would have denied the possibility.

So what has your mouth been testifying to? Have you been rehearsing the facts and denying the "spiritual laws of flight" available to you? Have you been waiting for God to do something when He has already put the power of blessing and life in your mouth? The words you choose to speak with your tongue are creating and shaping your future. If you're thinking, "That's too easy," then you obviously have never tried to control your tongue. Instead, speak good things when people speak evil of you. Speak life when the news is reporting death and darkness. Speak peace in the face of any storm, and speak your good future when a broken past says, "Nothing ever changes." Speak it all in the Name of Jesus, and those words will be the answer that brings joy (Proverbs 15:23).

BIBLE FOCUS — PROVERBS 15:4

"A gentle tongue [with its healing power] is a tree of life; but willful contrariness in it breaks down the spirit." AMP

PRAY THE WORD

Father God, You put power in my tongue, and I desire to speak life with it. Help me to overcome any carnal impulses to use my words for unprofitable talk. Your Spirit is in me, so let life flow from my mouth and the fruit of my words will not only bless me, but everyone around me. In Jesus' Name. Amen.

But I'm ugly and I don't have
wings - are you sure I'll grow
up to be like you?

BORN TO WIN

Everybody wants to win and succeed in life. So how do we define winning? In this world some people are labeled as winners while their personal lives are a ruin of moral and emotional failure. This is not God's idea of success. 3 John 2 says, *"Beloved, I wish above all things that you may prosper and be in health, even as your soul prospers."* God's plan for your success is an intricate design that correlates with every aspect of your life for total advancement.

God paid the full price for you, making you a winner in Him. That makes it pretty basic from His point of view. You were born to win, and all the losing you've piled up in the backyard of your life can't change that truth. You are born to win! In the book of Genesis 1:26, *"God said, Let Us make mankind in Our image, after Our likeness, and let them have* complete authority over the fish of the sea, the birds of the air, the beasts, and over all of the earth, and over everything that creeps upon the earth." God is a winner and you are made in His image. He designed you to have authority and dominion. God designed you to win, and that's why something inside you hates to lose. You weren't made for it.

Look at Adam; the first man. When he sinned in Genesis chapter 3, he rebelled against God and brought spiritual death on himself, but it still took 930 years for him to die (Genesis 5:5). The curse, sin, and sickness are constantly acting like spiritual gravity pulling you to a losing stop. That sinful nature you inherited from your ultra-great grand daddy Adam is working against your original design to be a winner.

Jesus said in John 3:3, *"Unless a person is born again he cannot see or experience the Kingdom of God."* The Kingdom of God is basically God's way of doing things and being right. Winning! But back in chapter 1:12 it says, *"To as many as received Jesus, to them He gave the power to be the children of God."* Ha! Just when the devil thought he broke Adam's perfect design for all of eternity, God sent the second Adam (Jesus) and He bought us back our birthright. In Jesus we have that winning spiritual DNA. If you've put your trust in Jesus, you have received a spiritual blood transfusion. Galatians 2:20 says, *"It's no longer I that lives but Christ that lives in me."*

Saying that you've put your trust in God needs to be said with more than just a nonchalant attitude on your part. Proverbs 16:3 tells us to, *"Roll your works upon the Lord* [*commit and trust them wholly to Him; He will cause your thoughts to become agreeable to His will, and] so shall your plans be established and succeed.*" Our trust in God should be so aggressive that, like a pilot light ignites a supply of gas, the power of God's Spirit in us detonates with our agreement of His Word and...voilá...success. That is the word for God's will for your life — "success." Humanity has had thousands of years to be deceived into accepting life under the curse as the norm. It's not. Sin, sickness, failure, defeat, and death have nothing to do with what you were designed for. John 3:6 says, "*What is born of the flesh is flesh; and what is born of the Spirit is spirit.*" God is that Spirit, and so we know that if you're born of Him, it's Him in you. That is pure winning spiritual DNA.

BIBLE FOCUS — PROVERBS 16:3

"*Roll your works upon the Lord [commit and trust them wholly to Him; He will cause your thoughts to become agreeable to His will, and] so shall your plans be established and succeed.*" AMP

PRAY THE WORD

Lord, right now I commit to You all my projects, plans, and dreams. Everything that I'm working at I bring under Your Lordship. I want to have Your thoughts and directions on all these matters. Your will be done in my life as Your will is done in heaven. Let all my works be directed by You, established by You, and let them succeed, Lord. In Jesus' Name. Amen.

He was going on and on about
all he knows, when suddenly... he
just puffed up!

SHUT UP & BE COOL

I've met some people who think they know a lot. It's kind of amusing, but people like that tend to talk quite a bit. 1 Corinthians 8:1 says that mere knowledge causes people to be "puffed up," and that can give you a false estimate of yourself. Have you ever noticed that pride loves to blow its own horn? People can easily adapt an attitude of self-promotion, because, let's face it; if your hope is not in God, you're on your own. Don't get the wrong idea, though; knowledge is a very good thing.

Proverbs 1:7 says, *"The fear of the Lord is the beginning of knowledge."* There are all different kinds of knowledge. Eve was tempted with the knowledge of good and evil. In the King James Old Testament translations, having sex with someone was referred to as "knowing" that person. Of course, this was only on a physical level, but again, knowledge ranges from good to evil. The knowing of God and His Word is the ultimate pursuit, because the fruit of that knowledge is life in every area. If you don't understand how "knowledge" works, you can open your soul up to all kinds of twisted thinking that will destroy your life. Your eyes and ears are gateways to your soul; therefore, the things you let in those gateways are the building blocks you have to work with.

Here is how you can tell if you're filling your heart with the right knowledge. Proverbs 17:27 says, *"He or she who has knowledge spares their words, and a person of understanding has a cool spirit."* The knowledge of God will humble a person in the truest sense, and real humility is a blessing waiting to happen. Let's say that you're an undercover spy. You understand that if you can get the right intelligence (knowledge), you will be able to achieve your objective. Suddenly you gain knowledge of some powerful information, and that puts you in a strong place of confidence. Lots of people are speculating, and even the news media is making strong projections; but you know the truth. You don't have to talk on and on or try to convince people. You've got the inside track. You sit back and smile, because you know the truth.

Can you see that? You're like the James Bond of the spiritual world. As fun as that little analogy is, the enemies of 007 don't compare to the real-life threats one can face every day. The truth is that you can be "cool" because of who you know and what you understand. You know the King of kings, and you understand that God's Word never fails. You don't need to spill everything in your heart out into the streets. God's Word even tells us not to *"cast our pearls before swine"* (Matt. 7:6). True knowledge is precious and should be handled with understanding and respect. The power of God's knowledge in your heart will transform your life, and you will be living proof of the good and perfect will of God (Romans 12:1). So put your horn away, because it's Who you know that determines where you go.

BIBLE FOCUS — PROVERBS 17:27
"He who has knowledge spares his words, and a man of understanding has a cool spirit." AMP

PRAY THE WORD
Your Word convicts me, Father God. It helps me measure myself honestly and realize that You have much better plans for me. Continue to reveal Your Word to me that I might be a person of great understanding, and help me guard my mouth from speaking too much. In Jesus' Name. Amen.

I want to bless you...
can you handle the pressure?

CAN YOU FEEL THE PRESSURE?

There's a little coffee shop on the poor side of town, and one day an old beat up car pulls into the parking lot. A man in tired, wrinkled clothes gets out of his "Junker" and wanders toward the entrance. He's unshaven, dirty, and has smelled better on any other day of his life. The truth is, he's down to his last few dollars and is living out of his only home, his car. He's very hungry, so he is going to splurge on the 99-cent donut and coffee special.

As he is placing his order, a good-looking gentleman walks in dressed in an expensive suit with the complete manicured look. He exudes confidence and has an air of influence about him without even trying. The unusual part of our story is that this mystery prince quickly takes a keen interest in our untidy fella. The rich man's words are warm as he speaks to his new friend and automatically offers a handshake upon introductions. He doesn't seem distracted at all by the down-and-out man's appearance, his lack, or even his un-bathed smell. Our gentleman navigates to some mutual interest and pretty soon both are enjoying the conversation. At this point our broke, smelly guy is happy to have some interest from someone so successful, and after all the rejection he's had in his life, this is like water to a thirsty soul.

The picture can't stop here, though, because there's a life outside the coffee shop. What if we got you to play one of the characters in this story? You're the poor fellow with the old rattletrap car, in desperate need of a bath and some new clothes. You've talked to your new friend for over an hour. He has listened to you, never once hinted at condemning you for your present circumstance, and shown you nothing but kindness. Strangely, you recognize that he sees value in you, and now he wants to leave the coffee shop. Your new wealthy friend wants to take you for lunch someplace nice and talk about your future. He offers a great place downtown with a view of the harbor. You've barely even heard of such a place, let alone imagined going there. The pressure is on. Can you feel it?

Abundance always puts pressure on lack just as goodness puts pressure on badness. The way you appear in this story is bad enough, but standing beside this prince, you are totally undone. If you have exercised your imagination and seen yourself in this story, you've wondered how to answer this invitation to lunch. Maybe it's more complicated than you had once hoped. Would you consider lying and telling him you have an appointment? Pride will always make you play the "shame" card. If you think it's impossible to be in this situation and walk in pride, you've been deceived. Proverbs 18:12 says, *"Before destruction the heart of man is haughty, and before honor is humility."*

The True Prince that has walked into your life is Jesus. His plan for you is honor, but to walk out that door with Him is to humble yourself and submit to His goodness. Believe it or not, many times we choose to lie and distance ourselves from His invitation. We want to change ourselves first and then go for lunch with the King. It can never work that way, because only He can take you and change you; otherwise you're just faking it. Pride fakes it. Decide today that you can handle the pressure. Humble yourself and go with the Prince. Your lack will be apparent each step of the way, but He will abundantly help you and provide for you. The pressure's on and that's a very, good thing.

BIBLE FOCUS — PROVERBS 18:12
"Before destruction the heart of man is haughty, and before honour is humility." KJV

PRAY THE WORD
Keep me from pride and arrogance, God. Don't let my heart be deceived by these destructive forces. Show me what true humility is, and help me to humble myself. You gave Your Son Jesus for me, and I could never deny that honor is part of Your will for me. You've paid a great price for my life, Lord, and I want to go with You wherever You lead me. In Jesus' Name. Amen.

Wasn't me.

No Excuse Sir!

It started when I was just a little boy. My little brother Lindsay and I would be playing and having a great time when suddenly, something goes wrong, and the next thing you know, the lamp is broken. My Mom would march into the room wanting to know who did it, and for some reason, we both knew it was the other guy's fault. There were other times we would get in a fight, and he'd end up hurt. The curious thing was, while Lindsay stood there crying, I would be explaining to Mom how I *really* had *nothing* to do with it.

I've learned that the world is wired with a lot of those same childish instincts. People just naturally don't want to take responsibility. There are some who try to build a career by surrounding themselves with scapegoats. The problem with doing that is, there's no foundation to it. Anything built on a lie will come to sudden destruction, and that's in the Bible. God is looking for people who will take responsibility for their lives. It's called honesty, and nothing of value begins until we look in the mirror of truth admitting to what we see.

Proverbs 19:3 says, *"The foolishness of man subverts his way [ruins his affairs]; then his heart is resentful and frets against the Lord."* I've heard so many people blame God for the tragedies of this world. There are countries where the people believe the rats are gods so they give first dibs on the food and water to their "gods". The children in that same country are starving while the rats eat 80 percent of the grain. One of God's commandments is that you should have NO other gods before Him. His commandments are meant to save and bless your life. The world looks at that gaunt, little child and argues, "If God existed He'd do something." What a foolish and ignorant thing to believe. It's like living in a house completely wired with electricity, full of light fixtures ready to perform, power at the fuse box, but every night the switches are left in the off position. The resident angrily shakes his fist at the local electrical company and says, "Doesn't anyone care that I live in the dark?" God has already given us everything we'll ever need and more.

When Jesus died He willed everything that was His to us, and Jesus was given everything from God the Father. The cool thing about this is; God has raised Jesus from the dead and now He actually administrates His own will to us. That means you can't lose unless you choose to. If things get messed up, don't "fret" against the Lord or blame someone else for that matter. Take responsibility for failure, and get back to the real business at hand; being on the receiving end of Jesus' will. God's agenda isn't to decide whose fault it is, but His heart is to love you. God so loved you that He gave, and that means His part is done. What are you waiting for? Paul wrote in the book of Ephesians 1:17-19 a prayer that basically asks God to open your eyes to what He's already done. God has already done what you've been hoping He was going to do. If you're prone to excuses, chalk it up to foolishness and get over it. You've got way better things to do. You're a beneficiary of the Kingdom of God so act like it — live like it!

BIBLE FOCUS — PROVERBS 19:3

"The foolishness of man subverts his way [ruins his affairs];
then his heart is resentful and frets against the Lord." AMP

PRAY THE WORD

Father God, it's time that I take responsibility for the "stuff" that's wrong in my life. You're not interested in excuses, and I'm not interested in living in the ruins. You have loved me so much that You paid the price for my failures and the price for me to be blessed. I don't need excuses — I need You. Be exalted in my life, God. In Jesus' Name. Amen.

SPECIAL NOTE

Thank God for organizations like Mission of Mercy that go into countries all over the world and rescue hurting children. Not only do they feed and clothe these little ones, but they also impart vision into their lives with education, a home, and love. The majority of the staff that operate the missions, schools, hospitals, and orphanages are graduates themselves of these programs. Now that's taking responsibility and turning on the lights.

Canadian office: 877-485-5001 / www.missionofmercy.ca
U.S. Office: 800-864-0200 / www.missionofmercy.org

How about.... don't honk if
you love Jesus!

HONOR OR STRIFE —
IT'S YOUR LIFE

There is a story in Genesis about a man named Abram who was very rich. He and his nephew Lot came into a new land with all their families, servants, and herds. They were so rich and large in size that the land could not hold both families. Things came to a head one day when a fight broke out between their herdsmen. Think of it as John Wayne's cowboys getting into a fight with the neighboring ranch hands over grazing territory. It was a big issue because good food and water for your herd, translated into a very healthy bank account. Abram turned to Lot and said, "Let there be no strife between us or our herdsmen because we're family...the whole land is before us, if you want the left, I'll take the right; if you want the right, I'll take the left" (Genesis 13:8,9).

In ancient Middle East culture it was understood that the eldest of the family got preference, but here is Abram giving that privilege to Lot. Abram was an honorable man. The nephew chose the better piece of land offered. The Bible says it was like a lush garden. God blessed Abram for giving his nephew the best land. Lot ended up living in a city named Sodom that was destroyed shortly after he got there. Abram increased exceedingly and was very prosperous. Now the dictionary defines honor as "a keen sense of ethical conduct," but in a world of situational ethics, the social rules for conduct are all over the place. That puts people in extremely vulnerable places like Lot was.

A very wise man once told me that biblical honor is an act of our will in harmony with God's Word. It will trigger and release the very goodness of God in our life. To see honor in motion, let's look at Proverbs 20:3, where it says, *"It is an honor for a person to cease from strife and keep aloof from it, but every fool will quarrel."* That tells us that there is a reward for staying out of contention and conflict. Yes, there is a time to make war, and no one can use this as an excuse for the tolerance of evil. Don't stand idly by while the helpless are abused. Abram fought to save the innocent, but he honored God by staying out of strife with his family, friends and neighbors. That doesn't mean people have to be right to avoid conflict with them, it's an act of faith when you trust God to look after you. Look at Genesis 26 when Abe's son, Isaac, digs a well and some dishonest men came along claiming it was their water. The Bible says in verse 20 that these troublemakers did "strive" with Isaac's herdsmen. Isaac could have gotten into a full out war, but he didn't because he knew God was his provider.

He moved on. The truth is he had to dig a few more times before they left him alone, but God blessed him for being a peacemaker and walking in honor.

Anyone can quarrel or pitch a fit. But a person with eyes for the future and confidence in God's hand, discerns and avoids empty conflict to focus on eternal rewards. That's called "fighting the good fight of faith and overcoming evil with good". Make a decision today that you're not going to get into strife. Instead, focus on the pure, heaven-born possibilities that are yours, walking God's way...walking in honor.

BIBLE FOCUS — PROVERBS 20:3
"It is an honor for a man to cease from strife and keep aloof from it, but every fool will quarrel." AMP

PRAY THE WORD
God, I ask you to keep me from strife and foolish quarrels. I want to walk in honor, and You can show me how to do that in every situation. In Jesus' Name. Amen.

Normally I wouldn't do this, but
for some strange reason... I'm
going to grant your request.

FAVOR WITH THE KING

People of influence can make things happen. I mean, they can open doors for you effortlessly that otherwise would take dynamite to get you through. Ambitious people recognize this and so the chase for favor begins. Far more valuable than money, favor is like a high-grade currency that some work for, many would cheat for, and others even "sell their soul" for. The Bible has a lot to say about this powerful, yet invisible, force.

First of all, you should know that having favor is God's will for your life. You must know God's will before you can receive and walk in it. 1 Samuel 2:26 talks about Samuel growing up and says he was, *"in favor both with the Lord, and also with men."* Now take a look at Jesus, the ultimate man. Luke 2:52 says, *"And Jesus increased in wisdom and stature, and in favor with God and man.*" Let your heart grab on to this; God wants you to have favor with Him and people. In fact, God wants you to have so much of it that it's like a shield all around you; pulling in what's good and protecting you from what's bad (Psalm 5:12).

The Proverbs speak often of favor, and in chapter 21 the first verse says, *"The King's heart is in the hand of the Lord, as are the water-courses; He turns it whichever way He wills."* As you well know there are good kings and there are bad kings, but notice that God doesn't differentiate. Irrigation is an ancient process of channeling water to land that otherwise would be too dry to grow crops. God has always had a way of making a dry land blossom and bringing dead things to life. It's in His character. You may have a crooked mayor or an atheistic boss who hates your faith in Christ, and in your pursuit of going forward this "king" seems to be the gatekeeper. Trust God and pray His will be done.

You see, now you know it's God's will for you to have favor, you can pray specifically, "God your will be done here on earth as it is done in Heaven." Jesus never told us to pray about the mountain did He? Jesus taught His boys to "speak" to the mountain (Mark 11:23). Begin today to speak to the "mountain" that blocks the flow of favor from the King's heart. An ungodly Pharaoh favored Joseph and a wicked king favored Daniel. Don't wait another day for some "nice" person to replace a position you need favor from. Decide you're going after God's will, whether they like you or not. All authorities and positions are designed to serve God's purpose. That is why we're instructed to give honor to authorities set over us (1 Peter 2:13,14), not because the leader is necessarily good, but the office was originally meant to be just and right. It's like the commandment to honor your parents is not supposed to be a debate over how good they are or if they *deserve* honor. It's a law to strategically place you in the direct course of blessing. The king's heart is in the hand of the Lord. Now *you* speak the will of God. The irrigation ditches will turn on, and the flow of favor will rush toward His plans and purposes for you.

BIBLE FOCUS — PROVERBS 21:1
"The King's heart is in the hand of the Lord, as are the water-courses; He turns it whichever way He wills." AMP

PRAY THE WORD
God, it's Your will for me to have favor. The children of the King have favor, and that pleases You. In the Name of Jesus, I speak to the offices and industries that have to do with my life: let favor flow toward me according to the will of God my Father. Lord, bless these positions of honor and authority with the knowledge of You. In Jesus' Name. Amen.

RESPECT OF GOD

HUMILITY & THE REVERENT

THE RHL FACTOR

Has there ever been a time in your life when you desired riches? What about honor or the fullness of life? I believe that we all have desired them at some point or another. The last time you considered having these wonderful things may have been as a child, but once upon a time you dreamed, even if it was for just a moment. I know this to be true, because you were fashioned by God to have all of the above. Not only have you been made in the image of God, but Psalm 8 verse 5 adds *"You (God) have made man a little lower than God, and You (God) have crowned him with glory and honor."* Now that is totally amazing!!

Right now you may be examining yourself and doubting this Word, but it is the truth. Most likely, you are the one living the lie. The bad news is that we all have sinned, and that means we've missed the mark. Psalm 8 makes it clear what the actual mark is, *"crowned with glory and honor."* Remember the prodigal son? Just because he was living in the dirt with the hogs didn't mean that there was a much better place for him. A far better place where there was riches, honor, and life! Think about this: the whole time the prodigal son was spiraling down, a home waited for him full of all the blessings he could ever hope for and more.

When Jesus told the story of the "Prodigal son," the turning point was when the son came to himself. That is a humbling place to be. To realize your true identity and how far from the "mark" you've fallen with the contrasting goodness of your loving Father that's waiting for you to come home. Proverbs 22 verse 4 says, *"The reward of humility and the fear of the Lord is riches and honor and life."* That is God's Word—I call it the RHL factor.

Part of truly believing God is trusting there is a reward for coming home and submitting to the Father: riches, honor, and life. That's a very convicting truth, because if you find yourself lacking in any of these areas, it becomes a measuring stick you can use to quickly judge yourself by. Humility and the reverent, worshipful fear of the Lord are the highway numbers on the joyful and rewarding path home. So, is this a good day for you? According to the RHL Factor, it can be and it should be.

BIBLE FOCUS — PROVERBS 22:4

"By humility and the fear of the Lord are riches, and honour, and life." KJV

PRAY THE WORD

Lord, Your Word totally shakes up the religious mindset I had about things like riches, honor, and life. Now I see that it's Your will for me to have these things. I submit to You again and ask you to show me how to follow after You in humility and reverence. In Jesus' Name. Amen.

Anyone??

FREE LUNCH HERE!

Imagine with me; a man who lives on the streets of New York City. He is very thin, dirty, and poorly dressed. The quick conclusion of most who see him is, "here's a no-good bum." It may be easy for you to consider a solution to his problem, but the roots of his poverty go deep. A few dollars may actually compound his already self-destructive lifestyle. A sandwich could be a good thing depending on whether it feeds him or his chronic addiction to welfare and the debt he feels society owes him. You may say that God is this poor fellow's answer, and I would have to agree with you, but what form would God take in coming to him? God is Love, but even love must take some tangible shape.

So we feed this guy, but now what happens? The sandwich could just be putting off his inescapable destruction for another day, or it could bring just enough strength needed for him to hear the truth of how his life could be transformed. Proverbs 23 verse 12 says, *"Apply your mind to instruction and correction and your ears to words of knowledge."* To go from where you are today to any place better will require the application of instruction and correction.

We may easily be able to see that as truth for our poor friend in the slums of New York City, but do we recognize that for ourselves? I've seen older men and women of God who I admire, totally refuse wisdom. It may have been instruction on following a better diet to avoid future health problems or some instruction in wise financial dealings to reap a reward. I've marveled as they've turned down a gift from God and at the same time wondered how many times I've done the same thing.

Let's renew our commitment to apply our mind to instruction, receive correction, and open our ears to words of knowledge. A spiritual "welfare sandwich" is not what God paid for with the sacrifice of His Son Jesus. God lifts the poor from the dunghill to sit with princes. Maybe it's time we stop deceiving ourselves and recognize the man on the streets. It's you and me without Christ, His Word, His instruction, and yes, His correction. Sometimes we can get so busy walking the ditches and trying to justify our fight for survival that we'll ignore God's direction. It could be a simple instruction to forgive someone, but it will bring such rewards that nothing could compare. Take a hold of more than a free lunch. With all your strength, grab on to God's awesome instruction and watch your days transform before your eyes.

BIBLE FOCUS — PROVERBS 23:12

"Apply your mind to instruction and correction and your ears to words of knowledge." AMP

PRAY THE WORD

I want everything You have for me, Heavenly Father. That means I want to grab on to Your instruction and be willing to receive Your correction. Use Your Word and other people to bring these gifts into my life. Help me to be quick to hear so I can increase daily in knowledge. In Jesus' Name. Amen.

GOT HONEY?

sn't it interesting how you act when you *know* something?
When you gain knowledge of something to any degree,
you make some kind of decision. Let's say you've just
tasted brussels sprouts for the first time. That new
experience of tasting is knowledge on which you will make
a decision to either like or dislike the food. How about the
first time you fly in an airplane? I've heard some people say
they love flying, and others say they hope to never fly again
in their life. That definitely wouldn't work for me with all
the flying I have to do. Now of course we know that there
are extremely varied experiences that a person can have
flying, even for the first time. Just like there are many ways
to cook brussels sprouts and quite a range of skills when it
comes to preparation.

Proverbs 24 compares tasting honey with tasting wisdom.

Verse 13 and 14 say, *"My son, eat honey, because it is good, and the drippings of honey-comb are sweet to your taste. So shall you know skillful and godly Wisdom to be thus in your life; if you find it, then shall there be a future and a reward, and your hope and expectation shall not be cut off."* That's pretty straightforward. Maybe you've never tasted honey, but the Bible tells us that "tasting" wisdom will translate into knowledge, and *that* stuff is sweet. Then it says that *"if"* you find Wisdom and come to an actual "tasting" knowledge of it, there will be a reward and a future. You will realize your dreams. I think we can safely assume *that* is something everyone wants. Why then do so few people find this "honey-tasting-wisdom" that God instructs us to eat? Even James 1 verse 5 says, "If anyone lacks wisdom, let him ask of God who gives to everyone liberally..." There it is — free to all who ask, but still so many people are void of God's wisdom.

Let's try to understand why God's children don't seem to want to "taste" Wisdom. Have you ever been told, "Hey, you've got to try this, it's great"? You sample the dish or even worse, order it off the menu and "yuk." Not only do you avoid that food in the future, now you are leery of that person's recommendations. It's an issue of trust based on experience. There are some people I know that have had frightening experiences flying in an airplane. If I had rehearsed their trials over and over before being in an airplane myself, there's a good chance I would have never flown, and if I did, it would have been an extremely stressful trip. Their experience was tainted by some error on man's part or maybe bad weather, but that didn't make it a true flying experience, even by airline standards. God doesn't make mistakes and there are no flaws with His Wisdom—ever.

There are a lot of people that have little to no relationship with God and definitely aren't listening to His Word when it comes to His recommendations on the tasting of life. You and I have been given the power of choice, and as we experience God, we will confidently trust His advice on the menu of life. Taste the honey, because it is good and sweet. Taste God's wisdom, and you will know the flavor of hope, a future, rewards, and your dreams coming true. Honey can be in your home, on your table, and even on your plate, but you haven't come to the knowledge of its savor and virtue until you taste it.

BIBLE FOCUS — PROVERBS 24:13 & 14

"My son, eat honey, because it is good, and the drippings of honey-comb are sweet to your taste. So shall you know skillful and godly Wisdom to be thus to your life; if you find it, then shall there be a future and a reward, and your hope and expectation shall not be cut off." AMP

PRAY THE WORD

Dear God, there is a hunger in my life for more. I believe it is a desire You have put in my heart for Wisdom. The sure rewards of life, hope, and a future are all things that I want. I ask You for more Wisdom in the Name of Jesus. Amen.

Hidden Treasure

've always enjoyed a good story about searching for hidden treasure. There is something about the character of those that refuse to give up. Of course, there is also the excitement of uncovering the priceless treasure. A secret map or some kind of mysterious code is a "must have" ingredient for the making of this kind of adventure. This is one of the ways I see the Bible. It's God's Word and His testament; it's Wisdom, life, healing, and blessing. It truly is the *ultimate* treasure map.

Proverbs 25 verse 2 says, *"It is the glory of God to conceal a thing, but the glory of kings is to search out a thing."* Treasures are hidden to protect them from thieves and destruction. Do you know that the Word says, had the devil known God's intricate plan for salvation, he would have never slain Jesus. The amazing thing is that God had prophesied in detail the birth, torture, death, and resurrection of the Lord for centuries before it happened. Still, the enemy had no clue of the defeat coming down on him. The devil knows the letter of God's Word so well that he used his perversion of Scripture to tempt Jesus, but only God's breath can bring His Word to life.

The ultra cool thing is that unlimited treasures are hidden in God's Word, and only the Holy Spirit can reveal them to us. John 16:13 says, *"The Spirit of Truth will guide you into all the Truth...He will declare to you things that are to come."* What if you had a DVD in your hand with the cure to every disease, the solution to every mystery, and billions of dollars of undiscovered gold mines? The only problem is that it's still 30 years ago and there is no such thing as a DVD player. Ouch! So close and yet so far! Can you see that? God has made this awesome design where He has hidden His Kingdom in plain view.

Jesus quoted Isaiah when referring to those whose hearts were against Him and said in Matthew 13:14, *"You shall indeed hear but never understand; and you shall indeed see and never perceive."* God's secrets are for everyone, yet Proverbs 25 say's *"It's the glory of kings to search out a thing."* In Christ you are a king. All these years you've had the DVD with all the answers you've ever wanted right in your hand; God's revelation Word. I love the first chapter of Ephesians where it says, *"The God of our Lord Jesus give unto you the Spirit of Wisdom and Revelation."* I don't care how many times you roll that disc over in your hand or set it on top of your TV, you need the player designed to reveal what's on that disc. You need the person of the Holy Spirit to reveal to you God's Word. Get yourself a copy of the map, and welcome the presence of the only guide that can lead you to all Truth and every treasure. Have a great day!

BIBLE FOCUS — PROVERBS 25:2

"It is the glory of God to conceal a thing, but the glory of kings is to search out a thing." AMP

PRAY THE WORD

Thank you, Father God, for concealing the treasures of life for me. Any good parent would hide the inheritance in a safe place for their child. It's the nature of Your glory to cover and protect. Praise You, for You have made me a king and a priest in Christ Jesus. It is an honor to come in to Your presence where mysteries are revealed. I ask that Your Spirit breathe Your Word into my heart. All in the Name of Jesus. Amen.

Why can't I shake this guy?

THE CURSE OF THE MOMMY

ike the sparrow in her wandering, like the swallow in her flying, so the causeless curse does not alight" (Proverbs 26:2). Did you know that a swallow will migrate back and forth from North to South, up to distances of 5,000 miles and will always fly to the exact location of its previous nest. That is accuracy to the extreme. Now consider what God says when He tells us that "the curse" lands every bit as accurately.

The spiritual laws in God's Word are surer than the natural law of gravity. The Bible says that the iniquities of the fathers are visited to third and fourth generations. Iniquity is a driving force on the inside of us where sin is an act of breaking the law. I've heard some people say, "I was born this way" when referring to a nagging drive they struggle with. The truth is that we were all born in sin and iniquity. Just like California has these fault lines under its geographical surface, so we were born with, and even acquire through experience, fractures in our inner self. Too much pressure on the wrong piece of real estate, and the next thing you know we've got an earthquake. Have you ever felt that shaking in your life? Have you ever felt like the apostle Paul when he said in Romans 7:19, *"I fail to do the good deeds I desire to do, but the evil deeds that I do not desire to do are what I am doing."*

Religion will tell you that you need to discipline that unruly fault line right out of your life. Some people even get into punishing themselves in hopes to gain control of their sinful nature, but that is an arrogant notion. God heaped the punishment rightfully belonging to all people, on His only begotten Son Jesus. Jesus paid it all. Now, do we presume to think we can add to the price He paid or even independently suffer the penalty of our sin? That is the arrogance of false religion.

Isaiah 53 is a very popular portion of scripture and yet a very neglected truth. Verse 5 says, *"He (Jesus) was wounded for our transgressions, He was bruised for our iniquities..."* It goes on to say that, *"by His stripes we are healed."* The outward wounds of Jesus were to deal with your sin, but the inward bruising of Jesus was to deal with your iniquities. By faith we receive forgiveness for our sins through the bloody wounds Jesus suffered. Healing is ours based on the truth that Jesus bore our stripes on His back. He paid the price for your sins. Please grab a hold of this truth: the price has been paid for the curse that has landed on you, and you don't have to live with that driving iniquity on the inside. Jesus was bruised by the design of a loving

God so that you and I could be free from the curse and all its tentacles. Claim your rightful inheritance of freedom, and don't neglect one facet of how Jesus' Blood has set you free. Today is a brand new day for you, because you know the truth. Your life will never be the same.

Bible Focus — Proverbs 26:2
"Like the sparrow in her wandering, like the swallow in her flying, so the causeless curse does not alight." AMP

Pray the Word
God, it is so amazing when I think of Your great salvation that is mine in Christ. I let go of my old way of thinking, and I give up on my vain attempts to save myself. I have seen the curse at work in my life, but today I break its hold by faith in the bruising of Jesus. He bled outwardly for my sin and inwardly to deliver me from my iniquity. By His stripes I've been healed. Thank you God; today I'm free in Jesus' precious Name!

FIREY TRIALS

Rowing to the other side
... Hallelujah!

FIRE, GOLD & YOU

I love meeting people and getting to know the story of their lives. Different countries and different cultures can help make new introductions even more interesting. With all the traveling I've done and all the people I've had the pleasure of meeting, there seems to be a few common denominators. One of those being, that people always have a personal trial, test, or tribulation to speak of. They could be either facing it, just through it, or fresh on the other side; but people have tribulations.

Of course there is a vast degree of trials that people endure, but generally speaking, "the heat is on." Isaiah said in chapter 43:2, *"When you pass through the waters ... When you walk through the fire, you will not be burned."* Notice it says *"when"* and not "if." The great promise in this verse is that God says, *"I will be with you."*

If you're like me, I want to have more understanding and knowledge of what's going on in my life. I try to see what is happening from God's perspective. In the book of Proverbs chapter 27 verse 21 it says, *"As the refining pot for silver and the furnace for gold, so let a man be in his trial of praise."* The purpose of putting silver and gold to the heat is to get the impurities out of it. The reward is a much greater value on the refined metal. The same is true of us. There are so many self-help books out there today basically trying to tell you how to increase your value, and here in God's Word has been the real answer all the time.

I like how God compares these valuable elements to us. You see, you are very valuable to God. Yes, you may feel like a lump of ore, but God says you're His gold. Now when refining this chunk of gold, the smith doesn't just throw the rock in the fire or else all would be lost. He places the precious piece of gold into a pot especially designed to withstand the extreme heat. Nothing is lost, and He is in complete control of every step of the process. Silver has its refining pot, gold has its furnace, and your fireproof container is your praise. It protects you and at the same time allows the heat of life to draw the unprofitable elements out of your life.

Everyday there are opportunities to feel the heat even in small ways. You're driving down the highway, and someone cuts you off or signals you with the wrong finger when in heavy traffic. Do you react to the circumstance or respond to God? Are you drawn into the open flames, or do you go deeper into the safety of that place of worship? The heat is on regardless of who you are or your position. The real question today is where do you find yourself? I love Psalm 34 and it opens with this verse, *"I will bless the Lord at all times: His praise shall continually be in my mouth."* David the Psalmist knew about trials and pressure, but he understood the safe place of praise. Today as you walk the path of life, consider where you are and what's coming out of your mouth, because it really is your choice. It brands you as pure gold to use God's Words; so give a shout of praise today, tomorrow, and at all times.

BIBLE FOCUS — PROVERBS 27:21
"As the refining pot for silver and the furnace for gold; so is a man to his praise." KJV

PRAY THE WORD
God, You use the trials and "heat" I experience in life for my benefit. I give You praise and glory. Not only are You getting rid of the impurities in my life, but You're taking me through to great victories. You are my provider and my protector. I praise You Lord! You reward those who seek you diligently. In Jesus' Name. Amen.

Announcer: "And that's
the end of the game."

WHO'S IN THE HOUSE?

hen you're the wrong person in the wrong place, it can really make you feel insecure. The pressure of not belonging can be more of an internal driving force than the circumstance itself. I went to an NHL game with a couple of my friends up in Buffalo, New York. A few minutes before the end of the last period, I took off for the restroom hoping to beat the crowd. I passed the doorway marked "Women" and walked into the next entrance. I actually had walked into a stall when it occurred to me that I hadn't seen the typical "guy stuff" in this huge facility. In fact, there was different equipment then I had ever seen in this cubicle. I was in the women's restroom in a stadium that sat over 40,000 people and I just heard the horn blow for the end of the game. Ladies were coming! Lots of them! I definitely felt the strong sense of not belonging coming up on the inside of me as I heard many female voices converging on the first entrance. I ran for the other door that I had mistaken earlier for the men's entrance. It was a close call. Whew!

The point I'd like to make is that nobody was in that washroom telling me I was in the wrong place or asking me to leave. Still, when I recognized I didn't belong, there was a driving pressure from within to get out of there. Proverbs 28:1 says, *"The wicked flee when no man pursues them, but the righteous are bold as a lion."* There is a confidence in belonging. When you are a daughter or son in a good relationship with your father, you walk in and out of your father's house without any reservation. Boldly you enjoy all his home has to offer because you belong there. If you are a stranger, your heart beats fast, and you creep along because you know you're an intruder. The slightest sound makes you jump, and you have to be intensely aware of the quickest escape so that you can run if someone comes.

Who you believe you are makes all the difference. The Word of God says, *"As a man thinks in his heart so is he."* Are you constantly walking in fear with a sense of not belonging? Are your decisions motivated by fear, or are you falling back confidently on the free gift of righteousness you have in Jesus? Romans 5:17 declares, *"... Much more surely will those who receive [God's] overflowing grace and the free gift of righteousness reign as kings in life, through the one Man, Jesus Christ."* Did you catch that, or were you getting all religious on me? Those willing to receive God's grace, and the "free gift" of His rightness, will "reign as kings in life" through Jesus. Amazing!

Now I ask you, who are you on the inside? This is truly the deciding factor on where you stand in life. Are you a child of God, joint heirs with Jesus and righteous because He is? Or are you the stranger, out of place and constantly having to fake your way into every room because, deep down, you know you don't belong? Today your whole life can be revolutionized, but it must come from the inside out. Today you can receive Jesus' gift of righteousness, and based on this, you are God's son or daughter. Say, "In the Name of Jesus I'm a child of God, and therefore I can walk and live in His righteousness, bold as a lion." Now speak it over and over until it moves from your head to your heart. You should see the day you've just started.

BIBLE FOCUS — PROVERBS 28:1
"The wicked flee when no man pursues them, but the [uncompromisingly] righteous are bold as a lion." AMP

PRAY THE WORD
I am in Christ, and that makes me a new creature. God, I refuse to live on the run. Because of what You've done for me, I can be bold as a lion. My confidence is not in myself but in You. I have Your Name and I am Your child. Glory to God, I'm bold in Christ Jesus. Amen.

GOD'S 20/20

To be able to see is an amazing gift. What you see determines a lot of the most basic choices you make in life. What you look at over and over establishes to a great degree the way you think. Advertisers depend heavily on visual stimulation to sell their products. You're driving down the road, and you see a billboard for this cola drink on ice. Next thing you know, you're so thirsty that you're pulling over for the biggest, coldest cola you can get your hands on.

What you look at (or aren't looking at) is constantly shaping your future. Job said in chapter 31 verse 1, *"I have made a covenant with my eyes; how then can I look lustfully on a woman?"* Here's a guy that had the wisdom to realize that vision had everything to do with being blessed or not, so he actually made a personal contract with his eyes. If what you see with your physical eyes is so vital, then how much more important are the perceptions of your heart?

In Matthew 23 verses 15 to 24, Jesus is coming down on the religious leaders because of their hypocritical attitudes and their abuse of the people. Jesus said they were "blind guides" and "blind fools." He wasn't talking about their ability to see but rather the blindness of their hearts. Here's what Proverbs 29:18 has to say, *"Where there is no vision, the people perish; but he who keeps the law, blessed is he."* You've got be able to envision where you are going *in your heart* before you ever get there. From a successful business to a prosperous marriage, you have to have a vision of what's to be.

Joseph, the son of Israel, had a dream of being a world leader. His life looked like it was heading in the totally opposite direction though; sold into slavery and then in prison on rape charges. Still you can be sure of one thing, Joseph held onto the vision God had given him. That's why Joseph could endure the hardships of being a slave and the temptation of being seduced by a beautiful and powerful woman, he had a vision. People who have a vision keep the law. They're not living for the moment but for the prize and reward of seasons ahead.

Jeremiah 29:11 says that God is thinking good thoughts toward you; how to prosper you and bless you, but the key is the state of your heart. He needs access to your life, and that only comes by faith. Faith is the evidence of things unseen; God-inspired hopes. Without His vision and thoughts in your heart, Proverbs says you would die. You can apply that to every area of your life: your marriage, your career, your health, and your finances. Examine your heart today, and even better, pray like David did in Psalm 139:23,24. *"Search me, Oh God, and know my heart ... and lead me in the way everlasting."* Today you'll be amazed as God leads you with His 20/20 vision.

BIBLE FOCUS — PROVERBS 29:18

"Where there is no vision, the people perish; but he that keepeth the law, happy is he." KJV

PRAY THE WORD

As I read Your Word, Lord, fill my heart with big vision. Help me to see by the Spirit so I'm not walking through life guided by what I see in the natural realm. You give me vision, Lord, and help me to keep the law of Your Word and the law of the land. I am blessed in Jesus' Name. Amen.

Yes ... we can protect you
and your loved ones.

GOD'S POLICY & HIS DEDUCTIBLE

Insurance is big business these days. People don't want to lose the little they have, so insurance brokers appeal to the public with campaigns that assure you that you're safe in their hands. The word "trust" is used along with one of our all time favorites, "security." Just think, for a premium of only a fraction of your monthly dollars, you'll finally be safe and secure. In your heart you know that's not true. With all the best intentions of any corporation, country, or creed this world operates within a broken system subject to the "laws of sin and death," Romans 8 says. That's why people who really need help, lose their coverage, because it's about the love of money, not about compassion or even mercy.

Now there is a perfect system, and it's called the "Kingdom of God." It's basically God's way of being and doing right. 1 John 5:4 says, *"For whatsoever is born of God overcomes the world; and this is the victory that overcomes the world, even our faith."* To overcome the law of sin and death that everyone is born under, you must have citizenship in a new Kingdom. To enter God's Kingdom you must be born again of the spirit, and that only happens by faith. Whatever you need from God comes into your life one way — by faith. It's God's bulletproof system to keep corruption out of the living contract He has made for you.

This is such an awesome policy! Let's make sure we understand how to receive these benefits. Faith is the key to receiving, and Hebrews 11:1 says, *"Now faith is the substance of things hoped for, the evidence of things not seen."* We also know that *"faith comes by hearing, and hearing by the word of God"* (Romans 10:17). You use faith whenever you carry a small piece of paper into a bank with your name and dollar amount on it. You don't see the cash when you hold that check in your hand, but if you know and trust the signer, you confidently make the trip to the bank expecting money based on what's written on that paper. That's faith. You can't see the physical shape of a natural law with your eyes, but you can tangibly see its effect on people and things. That's how the law of the Spirit works, except it always brings life.

God made a contract with us. To complete the agreement, He had Jesus stand in our place so that there's no chance of a breach. It's a covenant that is eternal and secure, free to whoever will receive. Proverbs 30:5 says, *"Every word of God is pure: He is a shield unto them that put their trust in Him."* What a policy! His words are in front of you today and the fact that you're trusting in them is faith. Not only that, but God has given us His Holy Spirit who is our

Comforter and Counselor. He teaches us about the policy and helps us get all the benefits. Oh yeah, Jesus also paid the deductible, and that means we have no excuse for not accepting his help. It's time to realize the beauty of living with the shield of faith all around you. What an insurance policy!

Bible Focus — Proverbs 30:5

"Every word of God is pure: he is a shield unto them that put their trust in him." KJV

Pray the Word

I am dedicated to Your Word, God, because It's pure and full of life. When I read It, let it spring up with faith in my heart with understanding of what it is You're saying to me. You are my shield, and I confidently put my trust in You. In Jesus' Name. Amen.

Remember (stomach), you
serve me. I don't serve you.

A PAUPER OR A PRINCE

When God was first coming up with the blueprint for mankind He said, *"Let us make man in our image, after our own likeness: and let them have dominion..."* (Genesis 1:26). Psalm 8:6 says that God has made you to *"have dominion over the works of His hands."* To have dominion over something is to have supreme authority and absolute ownership of it. That's why it is a direct violation of your incredible design for you to be ruled by your appetites. Your body was meant to serve you and not for you to serve it. That's dangerous!

Adam messed up and didn't give us much of an example of how to walk in dominion. The truth is that Adam's sin short-circuited our authority, and so began thousands of years of men and woman living like slaves. The ground that was to serve us became our taskmaster as people labored just to get food. Now the second Adam, Jesus, was the perfect example of God's design. Because Jesus was sinless, He operated in the total authority of His "man" design, and that's why He based His legal right to perform miracles; not on being the Son of God, but "the Son of Man" (John 5:27).

Jesus walked in total dominion as the Father had first wanted for us. The wind and sea obeyed His voice; a fish brought money to pay the taxes for Jesus and His friends; the water held Him up when He walked on it; bread multiplied; fruitless trees died when He told them to, and the stories go on and on. Jesus served people, even in dieing for them but always exercised complete authority over things. Even demons did exactly what He told them to do.

Great for Him, right, but what about us? Through the death and resurrection of Jesus, we've been adopted into the family of God. I love how Romans 8 verse 15 says, *"You have not received a spirit of slavery...but the Spirit producing son ship."* It goes on to say that we're heirs of God the Father and joint heirs with Christ. You see Jesus is the Lord of all and He has made us kings and priests by His Blood (Revelation 5:10). Even when you work for a company, you have been given certain authorities to exercise within that organization and their sphere of influence. Brothers and sisters in Christ, Jesus is the King of kings and there is no end to His authority and dominion. You're not an employee with Him but a child of God and given every right of a son and daughter.

In Christ you are a king (Rev.1:6) and called to walk in His authority. When you read through Proverbs chapter 31 you find this counsel in verse 4 and 5; *"It is not for kings to drink wine, or for rulers to desire strong drink, lest they drink and forget the law and what it decrees, and pervert the justice due any of the afflicted."* Maybe you've always thought this part of God's Word has nothing to do with you. Life is often summed up in whom you believe yourself to be. Today your heart judges you as either a slave to this world or a child of the King —a pauper or a prince. This belief bares the fruit of what you do, whether good or bad; and how you think, small or big. The pauper mentality is forever at the mercy to satisfy the endless appetites of the flesh. On the other hand, the same topic of consideration for any child of royalty would be; what wisdom protects a leader from perverting justice?

If you have caught God's vision for your life, then your agenda has become all about His Kingdom and Its gain. Anyone ruled by an appetite, a desire, a trend, a fear, or even a freedom is living outside his or her design and destiny. A good king eats and drinks to get strength so that he or she can be profitable in kingdom business. You are a king, and today is your day to exercise dominion. Take authority over your own life in Jesus' Name, and live above the curse.

BIBLE FOCUS — PROVERBS 31:4 & 5
"...It is not for kings to drink wine, or for rulers to desire strong drink, lest they drink and forget the law and what it decrees, and pervert the justice due any of the afflicted." AMP

PRAY THE WORD
Father God, its Christ in me that is the hope of glory. The evidence of Your goodness and Name in my life is what leads others to real change. Help me to fill my life with You so that love overflows to those around me, especially the afflicted and helpless. You have recreated me in Christ Jesus so I do not have to be led by my physical appetites anymore. The Spirit of God leads me, so I fulfill the laws of kindness and mercy. In Jesus' Name. Amen.

NOTES:

If you've enjoyed the fun illustrations by Ron
Wheeler, you may wish to contact him at:

WWW.CARTOONWORKS.COM
RON@CARTOONWORKS.COM

You might be interested in e-mailing the designer of
both the cover and the inside pages of this book at:

LINDSAYGRAPHICS@SYMPATICO.CA

BOOKING INFORMATION

If you're interested in having Stephen Marshall visit or perform in your area, please go to Stephen's web address below.

Visit Stephen's website for updates on his tour schedule, browse available products such as his recent CD release, or to contact him. Stephen would enjoy hearing from you at:

WWW.STEPHENMARSHALL.NET

ABOUT STEPHEN MARSHALL

Stephen Marshall is an acclaimed songwriter, popular singer and award-winning producer. A trained jazz/rock guitarist, he puts music to deep, yet simple, prolific truths that have changed the lives of people worldwide!

Born in the Province of New Brunswick, Canada, Stephen's journey through life has covered many miles and experiences that could have been a breeding ground for bitterness and defeat. Instead, his life is full of love, increase, and victory!

When he was a young boy, his father left the family. Stephen, his brother Lindsay, and his sister Angela will never forget that one day that changed their life forever. As their dad ran into the arms of alcohol and drugs trying to escape from hurts and demons in his own life, their mom ran into the arms of the all redeeming God.

She spoke life into her children. She told them, "God will be your Father. You can talk to Him! He will meet all your needs. He will answer all your questions. He will provide for you! God will never leave you. He will lift you up!" Stephen believed those words.

He started to write songs that released and expressed the emotions in his heart that he could not speak otherwise. From the beginning his gift for music and crafting lyrics was evident. The songs moved people's hearts as they experienced not just the music but also a story in the making.

In his early teens Stephen and his brother started a band with a couple of friends. They quickly became popular, taking the band on the road to youth groups, schools, auditoriums, and churches all over Canada, all while still going to school. This was the road that would soon take him around the world.

Today you will hear Stephen on radio, television, in concerts, or leading one of his self-penned songs, like *"Glory Glory,"* at a worship event. He is privileged to be all over this planet proclaiming through music, word, and media that GOD can *and will* turn the curse into a blessing! He is living proof.

Stephen currently resides in Brentwood, Tennessee with his wife Pam Thum who is an international Gospel singer/songwriter.

HERE ARE A COUPLE OF STEVE'S FAVORITE BOOKS BY DR. DAVE WILLIAMS

For a catalog of Decapolis Publishing products and Dave Williams materials, please call 800.888.7284, or write to Decapolis Publishing at 202 South Creyts Road, Lansing, Michigan 48917. You may also check them out on the web at **www.mounthopechurch.org** and go to the Hope Store to view product offers.